D1309795

If you were me and lived in...
INDIA

A Child's Introduction to Cultures Around the World

Carole P. Roman

To Remi- My very first fan!

And to his mom, Shilpa- thank you for all your support.

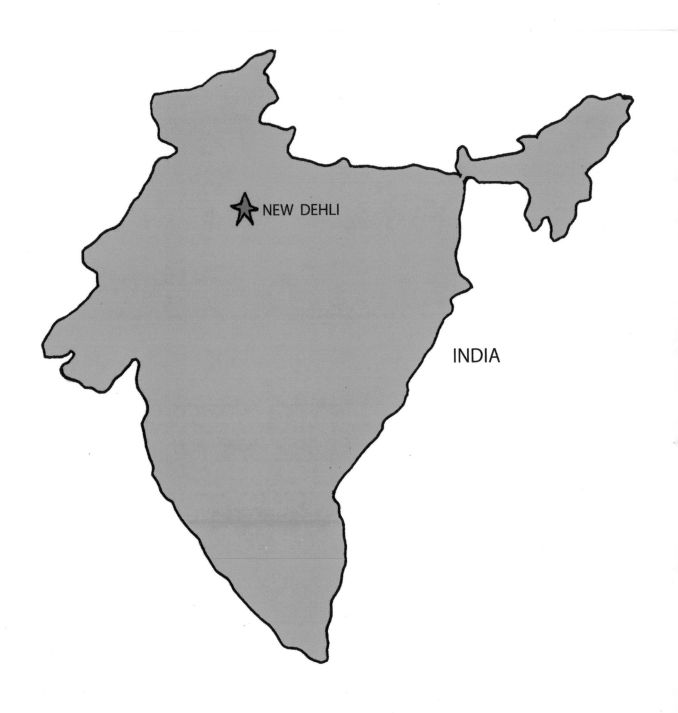

If you were me and lived in India (In-dee-a), your home would be in South Asia, where the map is a brighter green. It is the second most populated country in the world. That means a lot of people live there, and it is very crowded.

You might live in the capital, New Delhi (New Del-ee), a very important city where all the laws are made. It is built over the site of seven ancient cities. You might use a green and yellow rickshaw taxi to get around. There are over one hundred different languages spoken there.

If you are a boy, your parents could have named you Raj (R-aa-j), Rakesh (R-ah-kej-sh), or Anoop (A-noop). Little girls are often named Rhea (R-ee-uh), Priyanka (Pri-unk-a), or Nikita (Knee-key-ta) in India.

When you talk to your mommy, you would call her Maaji (M-aa-jee). Then when you need your daddy, you would say, "Pitaji!" (P-it-ah-jee).

An Indian rupee (r-oo-pee) is what you would use to pay to see a movie in a theater. Hundreds of movies are made there and the industry is called Bollywood (Bol-lee- wood). You would love the singing, dancing, and action in these exciting films.

When visitors come, you might want to take them to the Taj Mahal (T-aa-j Mah-hah-al). The Taj Mahal is a beautiful monument emperor Shah Jehan (Sh-ah Gee-han) made for his wife. Thousands of people go to India to see it. It is made out of white marble and has jewels pressed into its walls. You may prefer to visit Rajasthan (R-aa-j-as-th-an). It is filled with forts, palaces, and museums that were built by maharajas (mah-hah-ra-jas) and maharanis (mar-hah-ra-nees), which is what you would call kings and queens in India. You would travel through the Thar (Th-ar) Desert on a camel or in a jeep.

Because there are so many different cultures in India, there is a wide variety of food choices. If you were me, you would love spicy things. One of your favorite dishes would be biryani (bir-ran-ee), which is rice with fish, eggs, meat, or just vegetables. Some people in India do not eat beef or pork, so there are ways to cook vegetables with interesting spices. Cumin (Coo-min), curry (cur-ree), cinnamon (sin-a-min), and chilies (chil-lees) are used in abundance to flavor the dishes. Every meal comes with naan (n-aa-n), which is a

tasty Indian bread. You would love to drink a sweet lassi (l-aa-see), which is a yogurt shake with fruit and sugar.

Everybody loves to watch and play cricket (crick-it). You might like to be one of the players on the round field. There are innings, and a bowler delivers a ball to the batsman. The batsman has to hit the ball far away. Do you know of another sport that is like that?

Holi (H-o-lee) is a beautiful two day celebration that you would love very much. You would dress all in white, just like everybody else. It is a day Indians celebrate good overcoming evil. They also honor spring harvest.

You would be in a group of people throwing colored powder and water at each other. There is a lot of dancing under sprinklers too. So you would come home tired and messy and happy from all the parties, dancing, and food.

You would share your stories when you got back to pathshala (pa-th-sha-la). Can you guess what that is?

So you see, if you were me, how life in India could really be.

Pronunciation Guide

Anoop (A-noop)- popular boy's name.

biryani (bir-ran-ee)- delicious dish of rice, vegetables, and meat.

Bollywood (Bol-lee- wood)- largest film producer in India.

chilies (chil-lees)- spicy chili.

cinnamon (sin-a-min)- flavorful spice.

cricket (crick-it)- popular ball game in India.

cumin (coo-min)- spice.

curry (cur-ree)- spice.

Holi (H-o-lee)- joyous celebration filled with dancing, singing, and celebrating colors by throwing bright powders at each other.

India (In-dee-a)- large country in South Asia.

lassi (l-aa-see)- sweet drink made from yogurt, fruit, and sugar.

Maaji (M-aa-jee)- Mommy.

maharajas (mar-har-ra-jas)- king.

maharanis (mar-hah-ra-nees)- queen.

naan (n-aa-n)- bread made from wheat flour.

New Deli (New Del-ee)- capital of India.

Nikita (Knee-key-ta)- popular girl's name.

pathshala (pa-th-sha-la)- school.

Pitaji (P-it-ah-jee).- Daddy.

Priyanka (Pri-unk-a)- popular girl's name.

Rajasthan (R-aa-j-as-th-an)- a region located in the North Western part of India.

Raj (R-aa-j)- popular boy's name.

Rakesh (R-ah-kej-sh)- popular boy's name.

Rhea (R-ee-uh)- popular girl's name.

rupee (r-oo-pee)- money.

Shah Jehan (Sh-ah Gee-han)-name of the king who billed the Taj Mahal.

Taj Mahal (T-aa-j Mah-hah-al)- famous marble monument built in the years 1632-1653.

Thar Desert (Th-ar)- also known as the Great Indian Desert found in the northwestern part of the country.

Made in the USA
Charleston, SC
11 February 2015